CALIFORNIA
NATIVE AM

SHASTA TRIBE

WITHDRAWN

by
Mary Null Boulé

Illustrated by
Daniel Liddell

CONTRA COSTA COUNTY LIBRARY
Merryant Publishing, Inc.
Vashon, WA 98070

Book Nineteen in a series of twenty-eight

This series is dedicated to Virginia Harding, whose editing expertise and friendship brought this project to fruition.

Library of Congress Catalog Card Number: 92-61897

ISBN: 1-877599-42-5

Copyright © 1992, Merryant Publishing

7615 S.W. 257th St., Vashon, WA 98070.

FOREWORD

Native American people of the United States are often living their lives away from major cities and away from what we call the mainstream of life. It is, then, interesting to learn of the important part these remote tribal members play in our everyday lives.

More than 60% of our foods come from the ancient Native American's diet. Farming methods of today also can be traced back to how tribal women grew crops of corn and grain. Many of our present day ideas of democracy have been taken from tribal governments. Even some 1,500 Native American words are found in our English language today.

Fur traders bought furs from tribal hunters for small amounts of money, sold them to Europeans and Asians for a great deal of money, and became rich. Using their money to buy land and to build office buildings, some traders started business corporations which are now the base of our country's economy.

There has never been enough credit given to these early Americans who took such good care of our country when it was still in their care. The time has come to realize tribal contributions to our society today and to give Native Americans not only the credit, but the respect due them.

Mary Boulé

A-frame cradle for girls; tule matting. Tubatulabal tribe.

3

GENERAL INFORMATION

Creation legends told by today's tribal people speak of how, very long ago, their creator placed them in a territory, where they became caretakers of that land and its animals. None of their ancient legends tells about the first Native Americans coming from another continent.

It is important to respect the different beliefs and theories, to learn from and seek the truth in all of them.

Villagers' tribal history lessons do not agree with the beliefs of anthropologists (scientific historians who study the habits and customs of humans).

Clues found by these scientists lead them to believe that ancient tribespeople came to North America from Asia during the Ice Age period some 20 to 35 thousand years ago. They feel these humans walked over a land strip in the Bering Straits, following animal herds who provided them with food.

Scientists' understanding of ancient people must come from studying clues; for example, tools, utensils, baskets, garbage discoveries, and stories they passed from one generation to the next.

California's Native Americans did not organize into large tribes. Instead they divided into tribelets, sometimes having as many as 250 people. Some tribelets had only one chief for each village.

From 20 to 100 people could be living in one village, which usually had several houses. In most cases, these groups of people were one family and were related to each other. From five to ten people of a family might live in one house. For instance, a mother, a father, two or three children, a grandmother, or aunt or daughter-in-law might live together.

Village members together would own the land important to them for their well-being. Their land might include oak trees with precious acorns, streams and rivers, and plants which were good to eat. Streams and rivers were especially important to a tribe's quality of life. Water drew animals to it; that meant more food for the tribe to eat. Fish were a good source of food, and traveling by boat was often easier than walking long distances. Water was needed in every part of tribal life.

Village and tribelet land was carefully guarded. Each group knew exactly where the boundaries of its land were found. Boundaries were known by landmarks such as mountains or rivers, or they might also be marked by poles planted in the ground. Some boundary lines were marked by rocks, or by objects placed there by tribal members. The size of a territory had to be large enough to supply food to every person living there.

The California tribes spoke many languages. Sometimes villages close together even had a problem understanding one another. This meant that each group had to be sure of the boundaries of other tribes around them when gathering food. It would not be wise to go against the boundaries and the customs of neighbors. The Native Americans found if they respected the boundaries of their neighbors, not so many wars had to be fought. California tribes, in spite of all their differences, were not as warlike as other tribes in our country.

Not only did the California tribes speak different languages, but their members also differed in size. Some tribes were very tall, almost six feet tall. The shortest people came from the Yuki tribe which had territory in what is now Mendocino County. They measured only about 5'2" tall. All Native Americans, regardless of size, had strong, straight black hair and dark brown eyes.

TRADE

Trading between tribes was an important part of life. Inland tribes had large animal hides that coastal tribes wanted. By trading the hides to coastal groups, inland tribes would receive fish and shells, which they in turn wanted. Coastal tribes also wanted minerals and rocks mined in the mountains by inland tribes. Obsidian rock from the northern mountains was especially wanted for arrowheads. There were, as well, several minerals, mined in the inland mountains, which could be made into the colorful body paints needed for religious ceremonies.

Southern tribes particularly wanted steatite from the Gabrielino tribe. Steatite, or soapstone, was a special metal which allowed heat to spread evenly through it. This made it a good choice to be used for cooking pots and flat frying pans. It could be carved into bowls because of its softness and could be decorated by carving designs into it. Steatite came from Catalina Island in the Coastal Gabrielino territory. Gabrielinos found steatite to be a fine trading item to offer for the acorns, deerskins, or obsidian stone they needed.

When people had no items to trade but needed something, they used small strings of shells for money. The small dentalium shells, which came from the far distant Northwest coast, had great value. Strings of dentalia usually served as money in the Northern California tribes, although some dentalia was used in the Central California tribes.

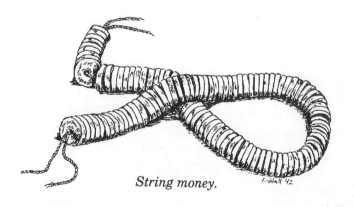

String money.

In southern California clam shells were broken and holes were bored through the center of each piece. Then the pieces were rounded and polished with sandstone and strung into strings for money. These were not thought to be as valuable as dentalia.

Strings of shell money were measured by tattoo marks on the trader's lower arm or hand.

Here is a sample of shell value:

> A house, three strings
> A fishing place, one to three strings
> Land with acorn-bearing oak trees, one to five strings

A great deal of rock and stone was traded among the tribes for making tools. Arrows had to have sharp-edged stone for tips. The best stone for arrow tips was obsidian (volcanic glass) because, when hit properly, it broke off into flakes with very sharp edges. California tribes considered obsidian to be the most valuable rock for trading.

Some tribes had craftsmen who made knives with wooden handles and obsidian blades. Often the handles were decorated with carvings. Such knives were good for trading purposes. Stone mortars and pestles, used by the women for grinding grains into flour, were good trading items.

BASKETS & POTTERY

California tribal women made beautiful baskets. The Pomo and Chumash baskets, what few are left, show us that the women of those tribes might have been some of the finest basketmakers in the world. Baskets were used for gathering and storing food, for carrying babies, and even for hauling water. In emergencies, such as flooding waters, sometimes children, women, and tribal belongings crossed the swollen rivers and streams in huge, woven baskets! Baskets were so tightly woven that not a drop of water could leak from them.

Baskets also made fine cooking pots. Very hot rocks were taken from a fire and tossed around inside baskets with a looped tree branch until food in the basket was cooked.

Most baskets were made to do a certain job, but some baskets were designed for their beauty alone and were excellent for trading. Older women of a tribe would teach young girls how to weave baskets.

Pottery was not used by many California tribes. What little there was seems to have been made by those tribes living near to the Navaho and Mohave tribes of Arizona, and it shows their style. For example, pottery of the California tribes did not have much decoration and was usually a dull red color. Designs were few and always in yellow.

Ohlone hunter wearing deerskin camouflage.

Long thin coils of clay were laid one on top the other. Then the coils were smoothed between a wooden paddle and a small stone to shape the bowl. Pottery from California Native Americans has been described as light weight and brittle (easily broken), probably because of the kind of clay soil found in California.

HUNTING & FISHING

Tribal men spent much of their time making hunting and fishing tools. Bows and arrows were built with great care, to make them shoot as accurately as possible. Carelessly made hunting weapons caused fewer animals to be killed and people then had less food to eat.

Bows made by men of Southern California tribes were made long and narrow. In the northern part of the state bows were a little shorter, thinner, and wider than those of their northern neighbors. Size and thickness of bows depended on the size trees growing in a tribe's territory. The strongest bows were wrapped with sinew, the name given to animal tendons. Sinew is strong and elastic like a rubber band.

Arrows were made in many sizes and shapes, depending on their use. For hunting larger animals, a two-piece arrow was used. The front piece of the arrow shaft was made so that it would remain in the animal, even if the back part was removed or broken off. The arrowhead, or point, was wrapped to the front piece of the shaft. This kind of arrow was also used in wars.

Young boys used a simple wooden arrow with the end sharpened to a point. With this they could hunt small animals like birds and rabbits. The older men of the tribe taught boys how to make their own arrows, how to aim properly, and how to repair broken weapons.

Tribal men spent many hours making and mending fishing nets. The string used in making nets often came from the fibers of plants. These fibers were twisted to make them strong and tough, then knotted into netting. Fences, or weirs, that had one small opening for fish, were built across streams. As the fish swam through the opening they would be caught in netting or harpooned by a waiting fisherman.

Hooks, if used at all, were cut from shells. Mostly hooks could be found when the men fished in large lakes or when catching trout in high mountain areas. Hooks were attached to heavy plant fiber string.

Dip nets, made of netting attached to branches that were bent into a circle, were used to catch fish swimming near shore. Dip nets had long handles so the fishermen could reach deep into the water.

Sometimes a mild poison was placed on the surface of shallow water. This confused the fish and caused them to float to the surface of the water, where they could be scooped up by a waiting fisherman. Not enough poison was used to make humans ill.

Not all fishing was done from the shore. California tribes used two kinds of boats when fishing. Canoes, dug out of one half a log, were useful for river fishing. These were square at each end, round on the bottom, and very heavy. Some of them were well-finished, often even having a carved seat in them.

Today we think of "balsa" as a very lightweight wood, but in Spanish, the word balsa means "raft". That is why Spanish explorers called the Native American canoes, made from tule reeds, "balsa" boats.

Balsa boats were made of bundled tule reeds and were used throughout most of California. They made into safe, lightweight boats for lake and river use. Usually the balsa canoe had a long, tightly tied bundle of tule for the boat bottom and one bundle for each side of the canoe. The front of the canoe was higher than the back. Balsa boats could be steered with a pole or with a paddle, like a raft.

Men did most of the fishing, women were in charge of gathering grasses, seeds, and acorns for food. After the food was collected, it was either eaten right away or made ready for winter storage.

Except for a few southern groups, California tribes had permanent villages where they lived most of the year. They also had food-gathering places they returned to each year to collect acorns, salt, fish, and other foods not found near their villages.

FOOD

Many different kinds of plant food grew wild in California in the days before white people arrived. Berries and other plant foods grew in the mountains. Forests offered the local tribes everything from pine nuts to animals.

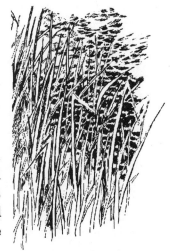

Native Americans found streams full of fish for much of the year. Inland fresh water lakes had large tule reeds growing along their shores. Tule could be eaten as food when plants were young and tender. More important, however, tule was used in making fabric for clothes and for building boats and houses. Tule was probably the most useful plant the California Native Americans found growing wild in their land.

Like all deserts, the one in southern California had little water or fish, but small animals and cactus plants made good food for the local tribes. They moved from place to place harvesting whatever was ripe. Tribal members always knew when and where to find the best food in their territory.

Acorns were the main source of food for all California tribes. Acorn flour was as important to the California Native Americans as wheat is to us today. Five types of California oak trees produced acorns that could be eaten. Those from black oak and tanbark oak seem to have been the favorite kinds.

Since some acorns tasted better than others, the tastiest ones were collected first. If harvest of the favorite acorn was poor some years, then less tasty acorns had to be eaten all winter long.

So important were acorns to California Indians that most tribes built their entire year around them. Acorn harvest marked the beginning of their calendar year. Winter was counted as so many months after acorn harvest, and summer was counted by the number of months before the next acorn harvest.

Acorn harvest ceremonies usually were the biggest events of the year. Most celebrations took place in mid-October and included dancing, feasts, games of chance, and reunions with relatives. Harvest festivals lasted for many days. They were a time of joy for everyone.

The annual acorn gathering lasted two to three weeks. Young boys climbed the oak trees to shake branches; some men used long poles to knock acorns to the ground. Women loaded the nuts into large cone-shaped burden baskets and carried them to a central place where they were put in the sun to dry.

Once the acorns were dried, the women carried them back to the tribe's permanent villages. There they lined special basket-like storage granaries with strong herbs to keep insects away, then stored the acorns inside. Granaries were placed on stilts to keep animals from getting into them and were kept beside tribal houses.

Preparing acorns for each meal was also the women's job. Shells were peeled by hitting the acorns with a stone hammer on an anvil (flat) stone. Meat from the nut was then laid on a stone mortar. A mortar was usually a large stone with a slight dip on its surface. Sometimes the mortar had a bottomless basket, called a hopper, glued to its top. This kept the acorn meat from sliding off the mortar as it was beaten.

The meat was then pounded with a long stone pestle. Acorn flour was scraped away from the hopper's sides with a soaproot fiber brush during this process.

From there the flour was put into an open-worked basket and sifted. A fine flour came through the bottom of the basket, while the larger pieces were put back in the mortar for more pounding.

The most important process came after the acorn flour was sifted. Acorn flour has a very bitter-tasting tannin in it. This bitter taste was removed by a method called leaching. Many tribes leached the flour by first scooping out a hollow in sand near water. The hollow was lined with leaves to keep the flour from washing away. A great deal of hot water was poured through the flour to wash out (leach) the bitterness. Sometimes the flour was put into a basket for the leaching process, instead of using sand and leaves.

Finally the acorn flour was ready to be cooked. To make mush, heated stones were placed in the basket with the flour. A looped tree branch or two long sticks were used to toss the hot rocks around so the basket would not burn. When the mush had boiled, it could be eaten. If the flour and water mixture was baked in an earthen oven, it became a kind of bread. Early explorers wrote that it was very tasty.

Historians have estimated that one family would eat from 1500 to 2000 pounds of acorn flour a year. One reason California native Americans did not have to plant seeds and raise crops was because there were so many acorns for them to harvest each year.

Whether they ate fish or shellfish or plant food or animal meat, nature supplied more than enough food for the Native Americans who lived in California long ago. Many believed their good fortune in having fine weather and plenty to eat came from being good to their gods.

RELIGION

Tribal members had strong beliefs in the power of spirits or gods around them. Each tribe was different, but all felt the importance of never making a spirit angry with them. For that reason a celebration to thank the spirit-gods for treating them well, took place before each food gathering and before each hunting trip, and after each food harvest.

Usually spiritual powers were thought to belong to birds or animals. Most California tribespeople felt bears were very wicked and should not be eaten. But Coyote seems to have been a kind leader who helped them if they were in trouble, even though he seems to have been a bit naughty at times. Eagle was thought to be very powerful and good to native Americans. In some tribes, Eagle was almost as powerful as Sun.

Tribes placed importance on different gods, according to the tribe's needs. Rain gods were the most important spirits to desert tribes. Weather gods, who might bring less rain or warmer temperatures, were important to northern tribes. A great many groups felt there were gods for each of the winds: North, South, East and West. The four directions were usually included in their ceremonial dances and were used as part of the decorations on baskets, pots, and even tools.

Animals were not only worshipped and believed to be spirit-gods, like Deer or Antelope, but tribal members felt there was a personal animal guardian for each one of them. If a tribal member had a deer as guardian, then that person could never kill a deer or eat deer meat.

California Native Americans believed in life after death. This made them very respectful of death and very fearful of angering a dead person. Once someone died, the name of the dead person could never again be said aloud. Since it was easy to accidentally say a name aloud, the name was usually given to a new baby. Then the dead person would not become angry.

Shamans were thought to be the keepers of religious beliefs and to have the ability to talk directly to spirit-gods. It was the job of a village shaman to cure sick people, and to speak to the gods about the needs of the people. Some tribes had several kinds of shamans in one village. One shaman did curing, one scared off evil spirits, while another took care of hunters.

Not all shamans were nice, so people greatly feared their power. However, if shamans had no luck curing sick people or did not bring good luck in hunting, the people could kill them. Most shamans were men, but in a few tribes, women were doctors.

Most California tribal myths have been lost to history because they were spoken and never written down. The legends were told and retold on winter nights around the home fires. Sadly, these were forgotten after the missionaries brought Christianity to California and moved tribal members into the missions.

A few stories still remain, however. It is thought by historians that northwest California tribes were the only ones not to have a myth on how they were created. They did not feel that the world was made and prepared for human beings. Instead, their few remaining stories usually tell of mountain peaks or rivers in their own territory.

The central California tribes had creation stories of a great flood where there was only water on earth. They tell of how man was made from a bit of mud that a turtle brought up from the bottom of the water.

Many southwest tribes believed there was a time of no sky or water. They told of two clouds appearing which finally became Sky and Earth.

Throughout California, however, all tribes had myths that told of Eagle as the leader, Coyote as chief assistant, and of less powerful spirits like Falcon or Hawk.

Costumes for religious ceremonies often imitated these animals they worshipped or feared. Much time was spent in making the dance costumes as beautiful as possible. Red woodpecker feathers were so brilliant a color they were used to decorate religious headdresses, necklaces, or belts. Deerskin clothing was fringed so shell beads could be attached to each thin strip of leather.

Eagle feathers were felt to be the most sacred of religious objects. Sometimes they were made into whole robes.

Religious feather charm.

Usually, though, the feathers were used just for decorations. All these costumes were valuable to the people of each tribe. The village chief was in charge of taking care of the costumes, and there was terrible punishment for stealing them. Clothing worn everyday was not fancy like costuming for rituals.

Willow bark skirt.

CLOTHING

Central and southern California's fine weather made regular clothes not really very important to the Native Americans. The children and men went naked most of the year, but most women wore a short apron-like skirt. These skirts were usually made in two pieces, front and back aprons, with fringes cut into the bottom edges. Often the skirt was made from the inner bark of trees, shredded and gathered on a cord. Sometimes the skirt was made from tule or grass.

In northern California and in rainy or windy weather elsewhere in the state, animal-skin blankets were worn by both men and women. They were used like a cape and wrapped around the body. Sometimes the cape was put over one shoulder and under the other arm, then tied in front. All kinds of skins were used; deer, otter, wildcat, but sea-otter fur was thought to be the best. If the skin was from a small animal, it was cut into strips and woven together into a fabric. At night the cape became a blanket to keep the person warm.

Because of the rainy weather in northern California, the women wore basket caps all the time. Women of the central and south tribes wore caps only when carrying heavy loads, where the forehead had to be used as support. Then a cap helped keep too much weight from being placed on the forehead.

Most California people went barefoot in their villages. For journeys into rough land, going to war, wood gathering, or in colder weather, the tribesmen in central and northwest California wore a one-piece soft shoe with no extra sole, which went high up on the leg.

Southern California tribespeople, however, wore sandals most of the time, wearing high, soled moccasins only when they traveled long distances or into the mountains. Leggings of skin were worn in snow, and moccasins were sometimes lined with grass for more comfort and warmth.

VILLAGE LIFE

Houses of the California tribes were made of materials found in their area. Usually they were round with domed roofs. Except for a few tribes, a house floor was dug into the earth a few feet. This was wise, for it made the home warmer in winter and cooler in summer. It also meant that less material was needed to make house walls.

Framework for the walls was made from bendable branches tied to support poles. Some frames of the houses were covered with earth and grass. Others were covered with large slabs of redwood or pine bark. Central California

Split-stick clapper, rhythm instrument. Hupa tribe.

villagers made large woven mats of tule reed to cover the tops and sides of houses. In the warmer southern area, brush and smaller pieces of bark were used for house walls.

Most California Native American villages had a building called a sweathouse, where the men could be found when they were not hunting, fishing or traveling. It was a very important place for the men, who used it rather like a clubhouse. They could sweat and then scrape themselves clean with curved ribs of deer. The sweathouse was smaller than a family house. Normally it had a center pole framework with a firepit on the ground next to the pole. When the fire was lit, some smoke was allowed to escape through a hole at the top of the roof; however, most was trapped inside the building. Smoke and heat were the main reasons for having a sweathouse. Both were believed to be a way to purify tribal members' bodies. Sweathouse walls were mainly hard-packed earth. The heat produced was not a steam heat but came from a wood-fed fire.

In the center of most villages was a large house that often had no walls, just a roof held up with poles. It was here that religious dances and rituals were held, or visitors were entertained.

Dances were enjoyed and were performed with great skill. Music, usually only rhythm instruments, accompanied the dances. For some reason California Native Americans did not use drums to create rhythms for their dances. Three different kinds of rattles were used by California tribes.

One type, split-clap sticks, created rhythm for dancing. These were usually a length of cane (a hollow stick) split in half lengthwise for about two-thirds of its length. The part still uncut was tightly wound with cord so it would not split all the way. The stick was held at the tied end in one hand and hit against the palm of the other hand to make its sound.

A pebble-filled moth cocoon made rhythm for shaman duties. These could range from calling on spirits to cure illnesses, to performing dances to bring rain. Probably the best sounds to beat rhythm for songs and dances came from bundles of deer hooves tied together on a stick. These rattles have a hollow, warm sound.

The only really "musical" instrument found in California was a flute made of reed that was played by blowing across the edge of one end. Melodies were not played on any of these instruments. Most North American Indians sang their songs rather than playing melodies on music instruments.

Special songs were sung for each event. There were songs for healing sick people, songs for success in hunting, war, or marriage. Women sang acorn-grinding songs and lullabies. Songs were sung in sorrow for the dead and during story-telling times. Group singing, with a leader, was the favorite kind of singing. Most songs were sung by all tribe members, but religious songs had to be sung by a special group. It was important that sacred songs not be changed through the years. If a mistake was made while singing sacred music, the singer could be punished, so only specially trained singers would sing ritual songs.

All songs were very short, some of them only 20 to 30 seconds long. They were made longer by repeating the melodies over and over, or by connecting several songs together. Songs usually told no story, just repeated words or phrases or syllables in patterns.

Song melodies used only one or two notes and harmony was never added. Perhaps that is why mission Indians, at those missions with musician priests, especially loved to sing harmony in the church choirs.

Songs and dances were good methods of passing rich tribal traditions on to the children. It was important to tribal adults that their children understand and love the tribe's heritage.

Children were truly wanted by parents in most tribes and new parents carefully watched their tiny babies day and night, to be sure they stayed warm and dry. Usually a newborn was strapped into a cradle and tied to the mother's back so she could continue to work, yet be near the baby at all times. In some tribes, older children took care of babies of cradle age during the day to give the mother time to do all her work, while grandmothers were often in charge of caring for toddlers.

Children were taught good behavior, traditions, and tribal rules from babyhood, although some tribes were stricter than others. Most of the time parents made their children obey. Young children could be lightly punished, but in many tribes those over six or seven years old were more severely punished if they did not follow the rules.

Just as children do today, Native American youngsters had childhood traditions they followed. For instance, one tribal tradition said that when a baby tooth came out, a child waited until dusk, faced the setting sun and threw the tooth to the west. There is no mention of a generous tooth fairy, however.

Tribal parents were worried that their offspring might not be strong and brave. Some tribes felt one way to make their children stronger was by forcing them to bathe in ice cold water, even in wintertime. Every once in a while, for example, Modoc children were awakened from sleep and taken to a cold lake or stream for a freezing bath.

But if freezing baths at night were hard on young Native Americans, their days were carefree and happy. Children were allowed to play all day, and some tribes felt children did not even have to come to dinner if they didn't want to. In those tribes, children could come to their houses to eat anytime of the day.

The games boys played are not too different from those played today. Swimming, hide and seek among the tule reeds, a form of tetherball with a mud ball tied to a pole, and willow-javelin throwing kept boys busy throughout the day.

Fathers made their sons small bows and arrows, so boys spent much time trying to improve their hunting skills. They practised shooting at frogs or chipmunks. The first animal any boy killed was not touched or eaten by him. Others would carry the kill home to be cooked and eaten by villagers. This tradition taught boys always to share food.

Another hunting tool for boys was a hollowed-out willow branch. This became like a modern day beanshooter, only the Native American boys shot juniper berries instead of beans. Slingshots made good hunting weapons, as well.

Girls and boys shared many games, but girls playing with each other had contests to see who could make a basket the fastest, or they played with dolls made of tule. Together, young boys and girls played a type of ring-around-the-rosie game, climbed mountains, or built mud houses.

As children grew older, the boys followed their fathers and the girls followed their mothers as the adults did their daily work. Children were not trained in the arts of hunting or basketmaking, however, until they became teenagers.

HISTORY

Spanish missionaries, led by Fray Junipero Serra, arrived in California in 1769 to build missions along the coast of California. By 1823, fifty years later, 21 missions had been founded. Almost all of them were very successful, and the Franciscan monks who ran them were proud of how many Native Americans became Christians.

However, all was not as the monks had planned it would be. Native American people had never been around the diseases European white men brought with them. As a result, they had no immunity to such illnesses as measles, small pox, or flu. Too many mission Indians died from white men's diseases.

Historians figure there were 300,000 Native Americans living in California before the missionaries came. The missions show records of 83,000 mission Indians during mission days. By the time the Mexicans took over the missions from the Spanish in 1834, only 20,000 remained alive.

The great California Gold Rush of 1849 was probably another big reason why many of the Native Americans died during that time. White men, staking their claim to tribal lands with gold upon it, thought nothing of killing any California tribesman who tried to keep and protect his territory. Fifty-thousand tribal members died from diseases, bullets, or starvation between the gold Rush Days and 1870. By 1910, only 17,000 California Indians remained.

Although the American government tried to set aside reservations (areas reserved for Native Americans), the land given to the Indians often was not good land. Worse yet, some of the land sacred to tribes, such as burial grounds, was taken over by white people and never given back.

Sadly, mission Indians, when they became Christians, forgot the proud heritage and beliefs they had followed for thousands of years. Many wonderful myths and songs they had passed from one generation to the next, on winter nights so long ago, have been lost forever.

Today some 100,000 people can claim California Native American ancestors, but few pure-blooded tribespeople remain. Our link with the Wanderers, who came from Asia so long ago, has been forever broken.

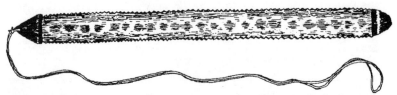

The bullroarer made a deep, loud sound when whirled above the player's head. Tipai tribe.

Villages were usually built beside a lake, stream, or river. Balsa canoes are on the shore. Tule reeds grow along the edge of the water and are drying on poles on the right side of the picture.

Women preparing food in baskets, sit on tule mats. Tule mats are being tied to the willow pole framework of a house being built by one of the men.

SHASTA TRIBE

INTRODUCTION

Little is known of the Shasta (Shas' tuh) tribe before the early 1800s, when White people arrived. The newcomers were fur traders who wrote about the Shasta tribe in their journals. Their writings, and those of other historians, show the tribe's population in the 1820s to have been somewhere around 2,000 people. Their writings also recorded the tribe's territorial boundaries.

There were four Shasta tribelets holding territory, at that time, in an area that is now in both California and Oregon. Three of those tribelets, or divisions, were in California, and they laid claim to the main rivers in that area: the Shasta, Scott, and Klamath. Using the names of those rivers, historians then named the three divisions of the Shasta tribe after them: the Shasta Valley, the Scott Valley, and the Klamath River tribelets.

Most Shasta land was 2,500 feet above sea level. It was mountainous and forested with evergreen trees. There were only two valleys, Scott and Shasta, that were below the 2,500 foot elevation.

Mountain ranges formed the north, west, and eastern boundaries of Shasta land. The southern boundary was marked with the Salmon and Scott mountain peaks.

All Shasta tribelets spoke the same language. Although they could understand each other, the Shasta tribelets had bitter feuds among themselves. Fortunately, in spite of the feuding, the tribelets also had good feelings about trading, sharing foods, and joining in the celebrations of their fellow tribal members. War was only a real problem when the Modoc tribe tried, every year, to bother Shasta tribespeople.

VILLAGES

Most important villages were found at the mouths of creeks emptying into the Klamath River. Village sites normally were on the edges of a valley, usually where a mountain stream flowed onto the valley floor. Research has shown there were at least 150 Shasta villages.

Mountain villages, where some people lived during the coldest part of the year, had several kinds of permanent buildings. Dwelling houses here were built in the shape of a rectangle. Some were as large, as 16 feet by 20 feet, since more than one family lived in them.

Permanent winter dwellings always were built facing water. They were dug into the ground about three feet and had steep, sloping roofs. Building took place in early summer, when the ground was not frozen, and neighbors helped with the construction.

Men put up the pole framework, while women tightly packed inside dirt walls. Women also formed, in the center of

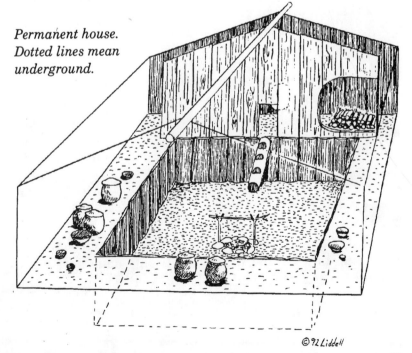

Permanent house. Dotted lines mean underground.

©92 Liddell

the house, the stone-lined fire pits needed for heating and cooking.

Roof rafters were placed around the top edge of a foundation hole, so only the roof was above ground. A house was warmer in the winter and cooler in the summer when it was built into the earth in this way.

Inside a permanent mountain house, wood stools and tule-mat pillows were used as furniture. Elkhide, deerhide, and sometimes even buffalo blankets were made into beds at night. Klamath River Shasta people also used raccoon-skin blankets for bedding.

Cooking and eating utensils were placed inside, in nooks beside the dwelling door. Clothing hung from roof rafters. Storage baskets and hide containers were kept on a shelf formed naturally at the edge of the foundation hole.

In the spring, mountain tribelets moved into brush shelters, staying there throughout the summer. In the fall, when acorns were ready for harvesting, families moved near oak groves and built single family bark houses. Families simply camped out in the mountains, in later autumn, when hunting took place.

Valley tribelets did not move about as much as the mountain tribelets. For most of the year, they lived in large round houses, big enough to hold several families. The dwellings had cone-shaped roofs made of wood planking. Floors of this kind of home also were dug into the ground about three feet.

Large villages had an assembly house built in the center of the settlement. Ceremonies and feasts took place in this building. The headman of a village planned the building, owned it, and lived there with his family. When a headman died, his son inherited the house. If only daughters were left, the house was burned. If a headman had no relatives at the time of his death, the assembly house was left to rot.

An assembly house was built like a dwelling house but was larger, usually 20 feet by 27 feet, and was built more than 6 feet into the ground. Framework for an assembly house included a ridgepole for the length of the roof and a center pole to support the ridgepole. The almost-flat roof and the above-ground sides were covered with packed dirt. Inside, the dirt sidewalls were covered with split boards.

Each division of settlements had an assembly house, and only the larger villages had sweathouses. For this reason, neighboring men, as well as men villagers, were allowed to use a sweathouse. These buildings were designed like an assembly house but were smaller, just large enough to allow 15 to 20 men in at one time.

Sweathouses were heated by central wood fires which gave off a dry heat. They were always built near a stream of water. Water had to be near so that when men finished sweating, they could jump into the stream's cold water to cool off.

Unique among all California tribes was another kind of Shasta sweathouse. Tribal men built small, domed sweathouses of willow pole framework covered with pine-bark slabs and animal hides, for their own families. Water was thrown onto very hot rocks, creating steam inside this kind of sweathouse. Both men and women in a family could use their sweathouse. Men felt sweating brought them good luck for hunting trips.

In villages that were large enough to have a sweathouse, men, young boys older than ten, single men, and visiting men slept there. If a village was too small to have its own sweathouse, men and boys slept in the dwelling house with the women, girls, and small children of their families.

Each man sweat at least once a day, believing that sweating purified his body. During the day, a sweathouse was also a place where men lounged or made and repaired weapons and nets. It was like a men's social club.

VILLAGE LIFE

Every village had its own territory and individual villagers owned their own fishing spots along the Klamath River. These spots were inherited from father to son. Families often owned a certain oak tree and their own acorn-gathering sites. The Shasta Valley tribelet could even own its own hunting places.

Large villages, and each of the three Shasta divisions, were led by headmen, who were in charge of keeping peace, advising their villagers, and settling disputes between villages. Headmen of the three California divisions, and the one Oregon division, were all equal in power. However, if trouble arose between any of the divisions, it was the Oregon headman who took over leadership to settle the problem.

When there were village problems, the headman of that area decided what a crime payment should be. If a criminal could not pay his fine, the headman had to pay. For this reason, it was important that a headman be wealthy.

If a serious crime, like murder, happened in the village, a headman acted as a judge, but other villagers were chosen to help decide punishment.

Because the punishment for all crime was the payment of a fine, each person and piece of property had a fixed value. Money was based on clam shell and dentalia-shell beads. Other objects of value a criminal could use to repay a victim were deerskins and woodpecker scalps.

Here is an example of Shasta values:

> Bride value:
> 1 to 2 deerskins, or
> 15 to 20 long dentalia shells, or
> 10 to 15 strings of clamshell disk beads, or
> 20 to 30 woodpecker scalps.

When a man wished to marry, he went to a person who knew the young woman he had chosen. This person spoke with the girl's father to decide upon a bride price. If a man could pay the agreed-upon bride price, the young bride was taken to the groom's village, where a large feast was given. After a short visit back at the bride's home, the couple went to live at the groom's village, where they built their own home.

If a bride had no brothers and the groom was from a family of several sons, the young man might choose to live at the bride's family home so he could help with hunting and fishing for the family's food. When a young man could not pay the bride price, he had to live with the bride's family and work for her father to pay off his debt.

Babies were born in a special birthing hut. In order to make sure their baby would be healthy and strong, the new parents carefully followed tribal rules. There were certain foods they were not allowed to eat, and new fathers could not go on hunting trips for a while after the birth of the child.

Children were named when they were a year old. A boy was named for some brave deed his father had done, or for the kind of job his father and grandfather had in the village. A girl was named for something her mother was known to do well. Poor parents who were not able to care for their baby, allowed relatives to adopt their child so it could have enough food and clothing.

In the Shasta Valley tribelet, people could give

An invitation string was given to invite people to a ceremony. The knots in the string represented the number of days until the event.

their names to others and take a new name for themselves (every person had to have a different name in this tribelet). When they did so, they were paid for their old names.

There were public ceremonies when a girl became a teenager. There were rituals the girl had to undergo, and a dance was given in her honor. Shasta people enjoyed this dance so much that it lasted from eight to ten days and was the most popular dance of the year.

Boys did not have a ceremony when they became teenagers. Instead, they were given the chance to go on a trip, alone, into nearby mountains. It was the boy's goal to search, during his trip, for symbolic signs assuring him of good luck in hunting and fishing in his future years.

If it was a winter ceremony, a boy only went for one day. In the spring, a boy's trip might last from four to six days. If the young man killed his first large animal during this trip, all the meat was given to an old man villager.

Shasta people believed that after death a soul traveled first east, then up to the sky. From there the soul went from east to west along the Milky Way, finally arriving at the home of Mockingbird in the afterworld.

Shasta people buried their dead, unless the death happened away from the home village. In that case, the body was cremated (burned), and the ashes were carried back for burial. Each family had its own burial plot.

All of a dead person's property was burned and buried with the corpse. In a Klamath tribelet village, a dead person's house was torn down and rebuilt unless that person had been a headman; then the house was burned. Shasta Valley people simply left the death house for a time, returning to it after the mourning period.

A widow cut all her hair off right after her husband's funeral. She also coated her head and face with charcoal and sticky tree pitch. A man who lost his wife (a widower) cut part of his hair off. There were also many taboos a widow or widower had to follow during a mourning period.

Both men and women had to avoid certain foods. For a certain length of time, women had to remain indoors, and men could not go on hunting and fishing trips. The name of a dead person could not be spoken aloud. If a villager forgot, and did say the name of the relative who had died, a fine had to be paid.

Warrior with pole vest for protection in battle.

WAR

Headmen never fought in wars but met with enemy headmen to work out peace matters. Trying to get revenge for the murder of one of its members, by someone from a neighboring village, could start a war between the two villages.

Another cause for war could be a headman from another village not accepting an invitation to a feast or ceremony. Wars could even start by one village fearing that witchcraft had been used on one of its villagers by another village's shaman.

33

Peace-settlement meetings were arranged after such an insult. These always took place in the daytime. Both groups dressed for war, and danced during the meeting. If an agreement was reached, the problem was settled with the paying of a fine, and with warriors putting down their weapons.

It was important to work out peaceful solutions to problems. War was cruel and not just a battle of warrior against warrior. Whole villages of people could be killed. If no peace could be arranged, war leaders were chosen by the warriors themselves, and all prepared for the fighting.

War was based on surprise attacks on enemy villages and on hand-to-hand combat. Men wore armor of either tough elkhide or vests made of small round sticks tied together with heavy vegetable fiber.

Women often went with warriors and fought the battle with knives, which they used to cut enemy bowstrings and to cut open arrow quivers. Winners of a battle took enemy scalps back to the victory dance at their own village.

RELIGION

Shasta people believed there were spiritual forces all around them, and these supernatural spirits caused all disease, death, and trouble that tribal members suffered. It was thought spirits lived in rocks, mountains, the sun, moon, and stars, and in many animals.

Because of this belief, if a villager became sick, or had bad luck, others were sure the reason was the fault of the sick person, for having angered the gods in some way. It was felt spirit-gods shot pains, icicle-like objects, into the bodies of bad villagers, making them ill.

Village doctors, or shamans, had the job of removing pain from a sick person. Almost all curing doctors were women in this tribe and got their positions by inheriting them from their mothers. Only one female doctor was allowed in a family at a time, however. A man did not become a doctor unless he had no sister to take over the job when his mother died.

All curing doctors were paid large fees before a curing ceremony could begin. If a sick villager died after a ceremony, the fee was returned to the dead person's relatives. When too many of a doctor's patients died, she could be killed by villagers.

Shastan curing doctors claimed to cure any sickness but colds. All women of the Shasta tribelets had great knowledge in curing sickness and injuries with wild herbs. Non-doctor women did their healing for free.

Although curing doctors were believed to be in close contact with spirits, they were more important as doctors than as religious leaders. One of the few big celebrations of the Shasta tribe was the ritual event of a doctor-making ceremony. This event lasted for several days and was held every five to eight years.

TRADE

Trading between other tribes helped the Shastans get objects they could not find in their own territory. Most Shasta trade was carried on with the Karok, Hupa, and Yurok tribes. However, they did get obsidian (volcanic glass) from the Achumawi tribe, and pine-nut necklaces from the Wintu tribe.

The large amount of buckskin they tanned, plus dentalia shells from Oregon Shastans and the Achumawi obsidian, gave California Shastans plenty with which to trade for acorns. When the Karoks, Hupas, and Yuroks came to trade, products from many other tribes were offered to them by the Shastans.

Sometimes trading went on at major events like the Karok White Deerskin Dance. Trading trails between the different tribes were well-worn from the constant travel of California Native American traders.

PLEASURE TIMES AND GAMES

Ring and pin game made of salmon vertebrae.

Myths were told more for children than adults and were not used to pass on tribal history. Myths were tales that had lessons in them about bad behavior and were usually about Coyote, who did both good and bad things in the stories.

Older women were the storytellers during the long winter evenings when myths were told. Children were made to repeat sentences of the stories over and over until they learned each myth.

Shasta tribal members had few musical instruments, most of them rhythm types of instruments used to accompany dancers. Deerhoof rattles, hide drums, and elder-branch, or bone, flutes that played only a few pitches made up a rhythm 'orchestra.' Music seems to have not been of as much importance to the Shastans as to other California tribes.

Children played with toys made from nature's materials around them. Acorn tops and buzzers, made from deer bone, were popular with youngsters. Both Shasta Valley adults and children used bark or wood buzzers. In the spring, young people played cat's cradle with a string during the first quarter of a new moon. This was thought to encourage the moon to grow bigger.

Shasta man of a Klamath River tribelet, in full costume. Buckskin shirt with dentalium shell and bead necklace, feather collar and head dress.

© 92 Liddell

Adults played the ring-and-pin game to pass time in December and January. The game was based on a myth about ten moons, of which five were killed. Most women enjoyed playing shinney outdoors, when it became warmer. This was a game like field hockey. Men played target games at that time of the year.

Games of chance were enjoyed. Women played a stick game of chance; men played the grass hand game where marked bones were hidden in nests of grass in team players' hands held behind their bodies, and the opposing team had to guess in which hand the marked bone was hidden.

FOOD

Game playing and other free-time activities, were only enjoyed in winter. Most of the rest of the year was spent gathering food and preparing it for storage so there would be food during cold weather.

Shasta people were fortunate, their territory was rich with plants, animals, and fish. The land provided many rabbits, birds, squirrels, and woodrats, all of them tasty. Deer, bear, and other large animals provided tribal people, not only with meat, but with warm clothing. Rivers and streams were full of salmon, trout, and eels. Even insects, like grasshoppers and crickets, were roasted for snacks.

Salmon, trout, and a few other fish were eaten fresh-cooked or sun-dried and stored. Animal meat was roasted over an open fire or baked in a stone-lined fire pit.

Acorns were the most important basic food of the Shasta diet. Acorns were eaten every day, and an effort was made to gather enough of them each autumn to last through one, and sometimes two, years. In years when the harvest was poor, acorns were received in trade from tribes in lower elevations.

Each year, thousands of pounds of these nuts were ground, leached (see Chapter One, page 12), and cooked into mush or bread for a single family's needs.

Besides acorns, the women gathered other nuts, seeds, bulbs, roots, plant leaves, and berries during the warmer months. A chewing gum was made from milkweed plants. Manzanita berries, when crushed, were made into a cider-like drink.

Wild berries were boiled and eaten with powdered grass seeds. Wild parsley was cooked by steaming, then was dried and molded into a block for storage. To prepare it for a meal, pieces were broken off the dried block and added to acorn or deerhoof soup as a seasoning.

GATHERING, HUNTING, AND FISHING

Tribal men hunted, fished, and built fires for their families. They helped women gather acorns and pine nuts. Women were in charge of all other food gathering and did all the carrying of water. Klamath River Shasta women also did woodgathering.

Men had many ways of catching animals for food. Single hunters would stalk deer and elk while wearing a real deerhead on their own heads. Some men were so good at moving like deer that they could walk right into a herd of the animals and get close enough to easily kill one of them with their bows and arrows.

Hunters also placed snares, nooses, and traps along the edges of animal trails mainly to trap and hold deer until they could return to kill the animals. Tribal hunters firmly believed that praying, going through ritual sweating, and following all tribal laws, would bring them good luck on a hunt. Many of them painted their bodies and performed dance rituals before going on a hunt to make sure they would find deer and kill as many as they needed.

When hunters worked in groups they could kill far more animals than a single hunter. Groups of hunters could chase whole herds of deer off a cliff. Hunters could divide themselves into groups, then chase the animals into a trap where the best hunters,with bows and arrows ready,awaited.

Young boys practiced their shooting skills on smaller animals like rabbits and squirrels. Later they were allowed to go on adult hunts. The first deer a boy ever killed was not eaten by him or his family but given to older villagers to enjoy.

The same river-fishing methods were used by nearly every California tribe. Important to all fishermen were many kinds of nets. Netting was made by men out of vegetable-fiber string or cord. Sticks of a certain length were used to make the squares between knots all the same size.

Shastans used large seine nets, that hung vertically in the water from stones tied to the bottom of a net and floats tied to the top. Seine nets were used to catch large fish. Dip nets, formed by attaching netting to a small branch bent into a circle, had long handles on them so they could be dipped deep into the water and haul fish up to a fisherman. In the spring, children dove into the river to scoop up mussels.

Traps woven like baskets were used at the openings in weirs, which were fences of brush or stone built across a small river or a stream. With the stream fenced, fish had nowhere to go but to the openings, where they were caught in traps. Spears with harpoon points were often used to catch salmon, as well.

No one was allowed to eat any fish until after the neighboring Karok tribe's White Deer Dance each year. Shasta people felt the Karoks performed the best first-fish ceremony, so many tribes in this area came to this Karok event.

A special ritual was performed at the dance, which had to be celebrated before any fish could be eaten. It was believed that if this ritual was not performed first, fishing would be poor all year. If anyone disobeyed this tribal law, he or she could be killed as punishment.

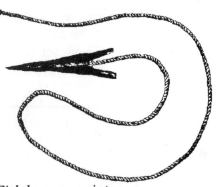

Fish harpoon point.

Tools for gathering plants included digging sticks for unearthing roots and bulbs, tall forked sticks for shaking oak branches to knock down acorns, and seed beaters for collecting seeds. Digging sticks were tough three-foot-tall sticks with very sharp points on at least one end. Not only were they used to dig bulbs from the ground but were also needed to dig the foundation holes for dwelling houses.

Obsidian knife blade.

TOOLS, WEAPONS, AND UTENSILS

Stone tools were made into grinding pestles, sharp-edged knife blades, heavy mauls or hammers, animal-hide scrapers, and arrow points. The stone which flaked best into pieces with sharp edges was obsidian, a volcanic glass. Obsidian was valuable enough to be counted as the kind of property which made a man wealthy in the eyes of his fellow villagers.

Animal-bone splinters were used as needles for sewing clothing together. Whistles and wedges could also be made from bone. Elk kneecaps and deer skulls were made into large spoons for men to eat with. Women used mussel shells for their spoons.

Wood was carved into spoons, awls (pointed objects to make holes in tanned hides or in wood), mortars and pestles to grind herbs, fire starters, bows and arrows, and container boxes.

Clever tribespeople made glue from fish scales, pine pitch, and cokeberry pitch. Some containers were made from rawhide. Cord and netting was made from the wild hemp plant. Deer snares were made from strong iris plant fiber.

Most canoes were received in trade from the Karok or Yurok tribes. Only the Shasta Valley tribelet made its own canoes from hollowed out sugar-pine logs. A few Shastas made rafts of bound tule canes.

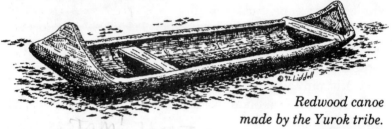

Redwood canoe made by the Yurok tribe.

Women of the Shasta tribe got most of their baskets in trade from other tribes. What few baskets they did make were woven by the twining method. Baskets were used as eating bowls, for collecting seeds, for food trays, hats, for storage, for collecting seeds, and even for cooking.

Weapons were made of stone, wood, and animal matter. Bows were shaped from wood to which sinew (stretchy animal tendons) was glued to make the wood more bendable. The more bendable a bow, the farther its arrows would fly. Bows were decorated with painted designs.

Some arrows were all one piece of wood, sharpened to a point at one end, with the point hardened by fire. This kind of arrow was good for boys learning to shoot with a bow and arrow, and was used by adults to kill small animals.

There were also arrows made from cane that had a front foreshaft , which fitted into the end of the main shaft. When this type of arrow was shot, only the foreshaft remained in the target, allowing the main shaft to be used again. These arrows had obsidian points attached to the foreshaft and were used to kill large animals like deer or elk.

Warriors used the cane arrows with stone tips for warfare, also. Rich hunters and warriors carried their arrows in quivers made from the whole hide of a small gray fox or an otter. Ordinary hunters made quivers from raccoon, wildcat, or fawn skins.

CLOTHING

Willow bark skirt.

Women of the Shasta tribe wore buckskin skirts and basket caps every day. Men wore buckskin hats, breech-cloth, and leggings. In cooler weather, men and women both wore deer- and bearskin-cape robes over their shoulders. During cold winter months, tribal men wore fur capes and leggings. Women in poorer tribelets wore skirts of shredded willow bark.

Shasta footwear was ankle-length buckskin moccasins for most of the year. Shasta Valley Shastas wore bootlength moccasins, and in winter added woven tule slippers. When walking in snow, tribal members used kite-shaped snowshoes.

Babies' heads were flattened by cradle boards when they were first born because the tribe felt a flattened head was beautiful. Pierced ears and noses were also thought to be marks of beauty. Women of this tribe wore tattoos of three wide chin stripes to show to which tribe they belonged.

Body paints were worn at ritual ceremonies. The paints were made by adding grease or bone marrow to red, white, yellow, or black pigment. Klamath River Shastans used a body powder of white chalk, while the Shasta Valley tribelet got their white powder from puff ball plants.

Ceremonial clothing was very colorful and fancy. Shamans (doctors) wore bright yellow hammer feather headbands; other women wore feathers at the sides of their heads. Woodpecker scalps worn by women had the bird bills removed.

Men also wore woodpecker-scalp headbands, but these scalps were complete with bills. Belts and very valuable dresses were decorated with the precious dentalia shells. Other ornaments were clamshell-disk necklaces, ear and nose decorations, pine nuts, bear teeth, bear claws, and bird claws.

Children of the Klamath River tribelet wore deerhoof necklaces. Often, belts woven from women's hair and buckskin were beaded with shell beads or porcupine quills.

HISTORY

Although the Shasta people first saw White trappers in the 1820s, they really had no contact with White people again until the Gold Rush in 1849. Gold miners, unlike trappers, wanted nothing to do with tribal people. They simply wanted to take over tribal land wherever they found gold on it.

The hard feelings caused by gold miners did not easily go away. Shastans from California went north to fight with Oregon Shastans in 1857, when territory disputes with settlers got fierce. These were such bitter battles that they are still called The Rogue River Indian Wars.

Survivors of the Rogue River wars were sent to different reservations. By 1870 the entire heritage of the Shastan tribes had been shattered. A tragedy, indeed.

SHASTA TRIBE
OUTLINE

I. Introduction
    A. Fur traders' writings
    B. Names of four Shasta tribelets
    C. Elevation of territory and boundaries
    D. Tribal language

II. Villages
    A. Sites of villages in valley
    B. Mountain villages
    C. Descriptions of mountain permanent houses
    D. Description of mountain food-gathering shelters
    E. Description of valley permanent homes
    F. Assembly house
        1. Who lived there
        2. Description
    G. Sweathouse
        1. Description
        2. Sweathouse use

III. Village life
    A. Owning property
    B. Headmen
        1. Amount of power
        2. Duties
    C. Crime and punishment
        1. Value of objects and people in 'money'
    D. Marriage
        1. Rituals and customs
    E. Childbirth
        1. Naming of child
    F. Teenage girls' ceremony and dance

G. Teenage boys' journeys into the mountains

H. Death and mourning customs and rituals

IV. War

    A. Reasons for war

    B. Peace settlements

    C. Kinds of battles

V. Religion

    A. Spirit-gods

    B. Shamans

        1. Curing rituals

VI. Trade

    A. Trading products

    B. Trading at ceremonies

VII. Pleasure times and games

    A. Myths

    B. Musical instruments

    C. Children's toys and games

    D. Adult games

VIII. Foods

    A. Kinds of food

        1. Acorns and other plant foods

        2. Animals and fish

    B. Food preparation and cooking

IX. Gathering, hunting, and fishing

    A. Men's jobs

        1. Hunting

        2. Fishing and nets

    B. Women's jobs

        1. Gathering plant food

            a. Tools used

X. Tools, weapons, and utensils
    A. Stone
    B. Bones
    C. Wood
    D. Glue, cord, and netting
    E. Weapons (bows and arrows)
    F. Baskets
XI. Clothing
    A. Everyday clothes
    B. Cool weather clothing
    D. Footwear
    E. Ceremonial clothes
XII. History
    A. Arrival of first white people
    B. Gold miners
    C. Battles with white settlers
        1. Rogue River wars
    D. 1870

GLOSSARY

AWL: a sharp, pointed tool used for making small holes in leather or wood

CEREMONY: a meeting of people to perform formal rituals for a special reason; like an awards ceremony to hand out trophies to those who earned honors

CHERT: rock which can be chipped off, or flaked, into pieces with sharp edges

COILED: a way of weaving baskets which looks like the basket is made of rope coils woven together

DIAMETER: the length of a straight line through the center of a circle

DOWN: soft, fluffy feathers

DROUGHT: a long period of time without water

DWELLING: a building where people live

FLETCHING: attaching feathers to the back end of an arrow to make the arrow travel in a straight line

GILL NET: a flat net hanging vertically in water to catch fish by their heads and gills

GRANARIES: basket-type storehouses for grains and nuts

HERITAGE: something passed down to people from their long-ago relatives

LEACHING: washing away a bitter taste by pouring water through foods like acorn meal

MORTAR: flat surface of wood or stone used for the grinding of grains or herbs with a pestle

PARCHING: to toast or shrivel with dry heat

PESTLE: a small stone club used to mash, pound, or grind in a mortar

PINOLE: flour made from ground corn

INDIAN RESERVATION: land set aside for Native Americans by the United States government

RITUAL: a ceremony that is always performed the same way

SEINE NET: a net which hangs vertically in the water, encircling and trapping fish when it is pulled together

SHAMAN: tribal religious men or women who use magic to cure illness and speak to spirit-gods

SINEW: stretchy animal tendons

STEATITE: a soft stone (soapstone) mined on Catalina Island by the Gabrielino tribe; used for cooking pots and bowls

TABOO: something a person is forbidden to do

TERRITORY: land owned by someone or by a group of people

TRADITION: the handing down of customs, rituals, and belief, by word of mouth or example, from generation to generation

TREE PITCH: a sticky substance found on evergreen tree bark

TWINING: a method of weaving baskets by twisting fibers, rather than coiling them around a support fiber

NATIVE AMERICAN WORDS
WE KNOW AND USE

PLANTS AND TREES
hickory
pecan
yucca
mesquite
saguaro

ANIMALS
caribou
chipmunk
cougar
jaguar
opossum
moose

STATES
Dakota – friend
Ohio – good river
Minnesota – waters that
   reflect the sky
Oregon – beautiful water
Nebraska – flat water
Arizona
Texas

FOODS
avocado
hominy
maize (corn)
persimmon
tapioca
succotash

GEOGRAPHY
bayou – marshy body of
   water
savannah – grassy plain
pasadena – valley

WEATHER
blizzard
Chinook (warm, dry wind)

FURNITURE
hammock

HOUSE
wigwam
wickiup
tepee
igloo

INVENTIONS
toboggan

BOATS
canoe
kayak

OTHER WORDS
caucus – group meeting
mugwump – loner politician
squaw – woman
papoose – baby

CLOTHING
moccasin
parka
mukluk – slipper
poncho

BIBLIOGRAPHY

Cressman, L. S. *Prehistory of the Far West*. Salt Lake City, Utah: University of Utah Press, 1977.

Geiger, Maynard, O.F.M., Ph.D. *The Indians of Mission Santa Barbara*. Santa Barbara, CA 93105: Franciscan Fathers, 1986.

Heizer, Robert F., volume editor. *Handbook of North American Indians; California, volume 8*. Washington, D.C.: Smithsonian Institute, 1978.

Heizer, Robert F. and Elsasser, Albert B. *The Natural World of the California Indians*. Berkeley and Los Angeles, CA; London, England: University of California Press, 1980.

Heizer, Robert F. and Whipple, M.A.. *The California Indians*. Berkeley and Los Angeles, CA; London, England: University of California Press, 1971.

Heuser, Iva. *California Indians*. PO Box 352, Camino, CA 95709: Sierra Media Systems, 1977.

Macfarlen, Allen and Paulette. *Handbook of American Indian Games*. 31 E. 2nd Street, Mineola, N.Y. 11501: Dover Publications, 1985.

Murphey, Edith Van Allen. *Indian Uses of Native Plants*. 603 W. Perkins Street, Ukiah, CA 95482: Mendocino County Historical Society, © renewal, 1987.

National Geographic Society. *The World of American Indians*. Washington, DC: National Geographic Society reprint, 1989.

Tunis, Edwin. *Indians*. 2231 West 110th Street, Cleveland, OH: The World Publishing Company, 1959.

Credits:
Pollard Group, Inc. Tacoma, Washington 98409
Dona McAdam, Mac on the Hill, Seattle, Washington 98109

Acknowledgements:
Kim Walters, Library Director, and Richard Buchen,
Research Librarian, Braun Library, Southwest Museum
Special thanks